Big Shiny Moon! What's in a Spaceship Space for Kids

Children's Aeronautics & Astronautics Books

Read on for
interesting
Moon and
spaceship
facts for kids!

The Moon is approximately 4.5 billion years old.

It is the
only natural
satellite in the
Solar System.

You can see the surface of the Moon using binoculars or a small telescope.

The Moon's surface shows the damage caused by rocks hitting it.

The first man to draw a proper map of the Moon was Galileo.

In 1959, Luna 1 was the first spacecraft to reach the Moon.

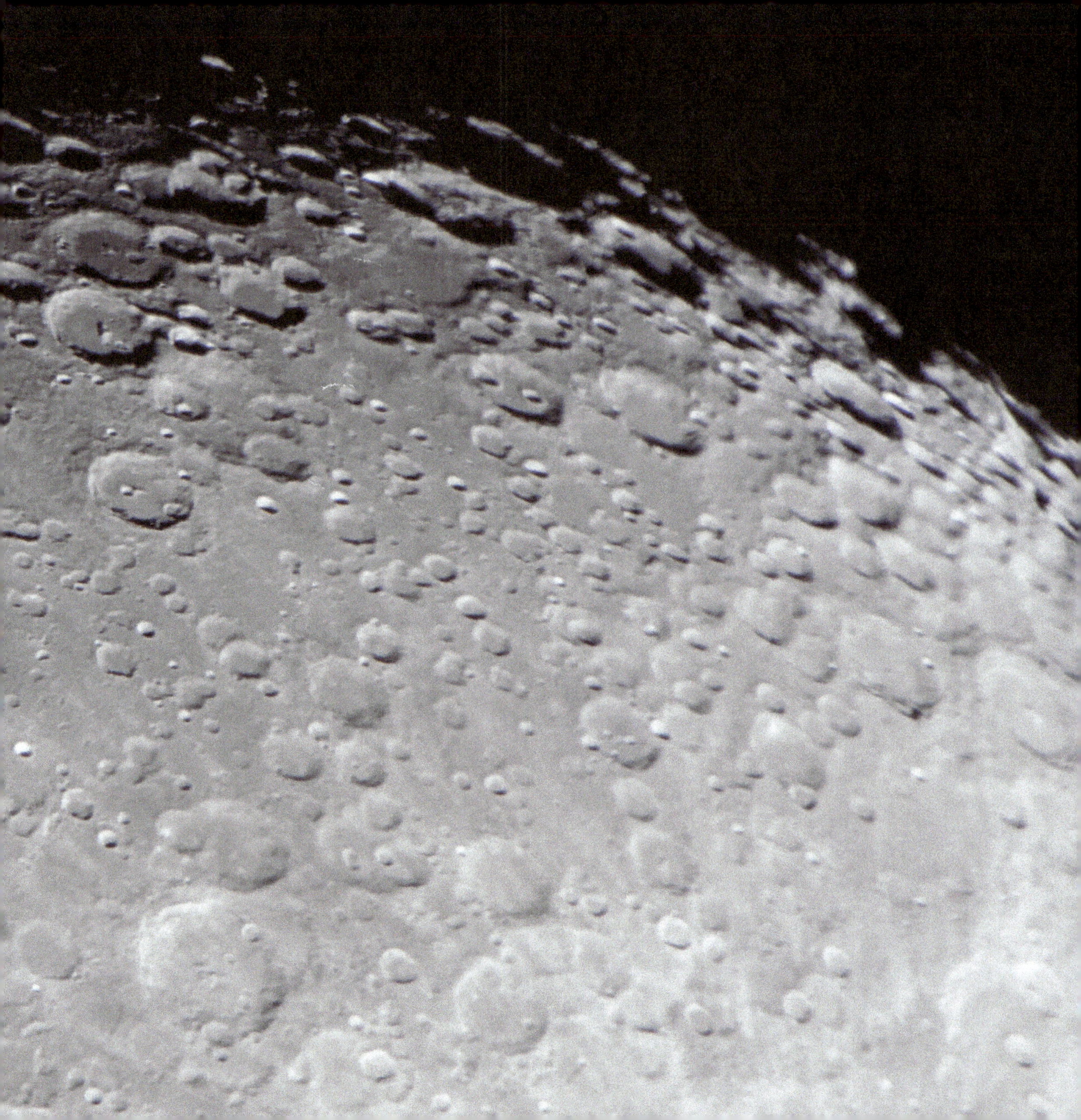

Neil Armstrong was the first person to land on the Moon.

The distance from the Moon to the Earth is 250,000 miles.

Holes in the Moon are called CRATERS.

The Moon orbits the Earth every 27.3 days.

Mons Huygens is the tallest mountain on the Moon, just over half of Mt Everest's height.

The side we see is called the near side of the Moon while the other side is called the far side.

The Moon is very cold at night but very hot during the day.

The Earth's tides are caused by the gravitational pull of the Moon.

The NASA Apollo 11 mission launched from the USA was the first manned Moon landing (1969).

Earth's gravity is much stronger than the Moons.

The Moon is said to be moving away from earth at about 3.8 cm every year.

Research
and learn
more about
the Moon!
Have fun!

Visit
BABY PROFESSOR
EDUCATION KIDS
www.BabyProfessorBooks.com
to download Free Baby Professor eBooks
and view our catalog of new and exciting
Children's Books

www.ingramcontent.com/pod-product-compliance
Lightning Source LLC
LaVergne TN
LVHW060830170826
845678LV00010B/1947
9798869443267